Time Series Databases
New Ways to Store and Access Data

Ted Dunning and Ellen Friedman

Beijing · Cambridge · Farnham · Köln · Sebastopol · Tokyo

Table of Contents

Preface

Time series databases enable a fundamental step in the central storage and analysis of many types of machine data. As such, they lie at the heart of the Internet of Things (IoT). There's a revolution in sensor-to-insight data flow that is rapidly changing the way we perceive and understand the world around us. Much of the data generated by sensors, as well as a variety of other sources, benefits from being collected as time series.

Although the idea of collecting and analyzing time series data is not new, the astounding scale of modern datasets, the velocity of data accumulation in many cases, and the variety of new data sources together contribute to making the current task of building scalable time series databases a huge challenge. A new world of time series data calls for new approaches and new tools.

In This Book

The huge volume of data to be handled by modern time series databases (TSDB) calls for scalability. Systems like Apache Cassandra, Apache HBase, MapR-DB, and other NoSQL databases are built for this scale, and they allow developers to scale relatively simple applications to extraordinary levels. In this book, we show you how to build scalable, high-performance time series databases using open source software on top of Apache HBase or MapR-DB. We focus on how to collect, store, and access large-scale time series data rather than the methods for analysis.

Chapter 1 explains the value of using time series data, and in Chapter 2 we present an overview of modern use cases as well as a comparison of relational databases (RDBMS) versus non-relational NoSQL databases in the context of time series data. Chapter 3 and Chapter 4 provide you with an explanation of the concepts involved in building a high-performance TSDB and a detailed examination of how to implement them. The remaining chapters explore some more advanced issues, including how time series databases contribute to practical machine learning and how to handle the added complexity of geo-temporal data.

The combination of conceptual explanation and technical implementation makes this book useful for a variety of audiences, from practitioners to business and project managers. To understand the implementation details, basic computer programming skills suffice; no special math or language experience is required.

We hope you enjoy this book.

CHAPTER 1

Time Series Data: Why Collect It?

*"Collect your data as if your life
depends on it!"*

This bold admonition may seem like a quote from an overzealous project manager who holds extreme views on work ethic, but in fact, sometimes your life *does* depend on how you collect your data. Time series data provides many such serious examples. But let's begin with something less life threatening, such as: where would you like to spend your vacation?

Suppose you've been living in Seattle, Washington for two years. You've enjoyed a lovely summer, but as the season moves into October, you are not looking forward to what you expect will once again be a gray, chilly, and wet winter. As a break, you decide to treat yourself to a short holiday in December to go someplace warm and sunny. Now begins the search for a good destination.

You want sunshine on your holiday, so you start by seeking out reports for rainfall in potential vacation places. Reasoning that an average of many measurements will provide a more accurate report than just checking what is happening at the moment, you compare the yearly rainfall average for the Caribbean country of Costa Rica (about 77 inches or 196 cm) with that of the South American coastal city of Rio de Janeiro, Brazil (46 inches or 117cm). Seeing that Costa Rica gets almost twice as much rain per year on average than Rio de Janeiro, you choose the Brazilian city for your December trip and end up slightly disappointed when it rains all four days of your holiday.

The probability of choosing a sunny destination for December might have been better if you had looked at rainfall measurements recorded with the time at which they were made throughout the year rather than just an annual average. A pattern of rainfall would be revealed, as shown in Figure 1-1. With this time series style of data collection, you could have easily seen that in December you were far more likely to have a sunny holiday in Costa Rica than in Rio, though that would certainly not have been true for a September trip.

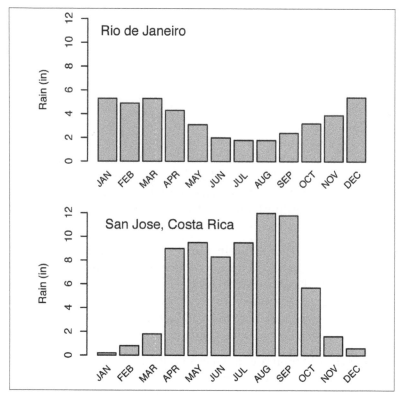

Figure 1-1. These graphs show the monthly rainfall measurements for Rio de Janeiro, Brazil, and San Jose, Costa Rica. Notice the sharp reduction in rainfall in Costa Rica going from September–October to December–January. Despite a higher average yearly rainfall in Costa Rica, its winter months of December and January are generally drier than those months in Rio de Janeiro (or for that matter, in Seattle).

This small-scale, lighthearted analogy hints at the useful insights possible when certain types of data are recorded as a time series—as measurements or observations of events as a function of the time at which they occurred. The variety of situations in which time series are useful is wide ranging and growing, especially as new technologies are producing more data of this type and as new tools are making it feasible to make use of time series data at large scale and in novel applications. As we alluded to at the start, recording the exact time at which a critical parameter was measured or a particular event occurred can have a big impact on some very serious situations such as safety and risk reduction. The airline industry is one such example.

Recording the time at which a measurement was made can greatly expand the value of the data being collected. We have all heard of the flight data recorders used in airplane travel as a way to reconstruct events after a malfunction or crash. Oddly enough, the public sometimes calls them "black boxes," although they are generally painted a bright color such as orange. A modern aircraft is equipped with sensors to measure and report data many times per second for dozens of parameters throughout the flight. These measurements include altitude, flight path, engine temperature and power, indicated air speed, fuel consumption, and control settings. Each measurement includes the time it was made. In the event of a crash or serious accident, the events and actions leading up to the crash can be reconstructed in exquisite detail from these data.

Flight sensor data is not only used to reconstruct events that precede a malfunction. Some of this sensor data is transferred to other systems for analysis of specific aspects of flight performance in order for the airline company to optimize operations and maintain safety standards and for the equipment manufacturers to track the behavior of specific components along with their microenvironment, such as vibration, temperature, or pressure. Analysis of these time series datasets can provide valuable insights that include how to improve fuel consumption, change recommended procedures to reduce risk, and how best to schedule maintenance and equipment replacement. Because the time of each measurement is recorded accurately, it's possible to correlate many different conditions and events. Figure 1-2 displays time series data, the altitude data from flight data systems of a number of aircraft taking off from San Jose, California.

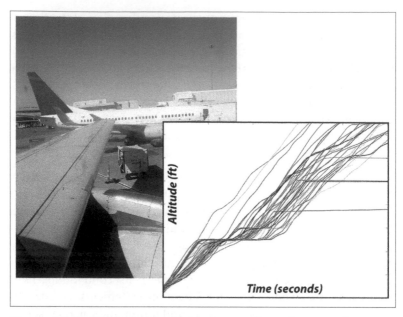

Figure 1-2. Dynamic systems such as aircraft produce a wide variety of data that can and should be stored as a time series to reap the maximum benefit from analytics, especially if the predominant access pattern for queries is based on a time range. The chart shows the first few minutes of altitude data from the flight data systems of aircraft taking off at a busy airport in California.

To clarify the concept of a time series, let's first consider a case where a time series is not necessary. Sometimes you just want to know the value of a particular parameter *at the current moment*. As a simple example, think about glancing at the speedometer in a car while driving. What's of interest in this situation is to know the speed at the moment, rather than having a history of how that condition has changed with time. In this case, a time series of speed measurements is not of interest to the driver.

Next, consider how you think about time. Going back to the analogy of a holiday flight for a moment, sometimes you are concerned with the length of a *time interval* --how long is the flight in hours, for instance. Once your flight arrives, your perception likely shifts to think of time as an *absolute reference*: your connecting flight leaves at 10:42 am, your meeting begins at 1:00 pm, etc. As you travel, time may also represent a *sequence*. Those people who arrive earlier than you in the taxi line are in front of you and catch a cab while you are still waiting.

Time as interval, as an ordering principle for a sequence, as absolute reference—all of these ways of thinking about time can also be useful in different contexts. Data collected as a time series is likely more useful than a single measurement when you are concerned with the absolute time at which a thing occurred or with the order in which particular events happened or with determining rates of change. But note that time series data tells you *when something happened*, not necessarily *when you learned about it*, because data may be recorded long after it is measured. (To tell when you knew certain information, you would need a bi-temporal database, which is beyond the scope of this book.) With time series data, not only can you determine the sequence in which events happened, you also can correlate different types of events or conditions that co-occur. You might want to know the temperature and vibrations in a piece of equipment on an airplane as well as the setting of specific controls at the time the measurements were made. By correlating different time series, you may be able to determine how these conditions correspond.

The basis of a time series is the repeated measurement of parameters over time together with the times at which the measurements were made. Time series often consist of measurements made at regular intervals, but the regularity of time intervals between measurements is not a requirement. Also, the data collected is very commonly a number, but again, that is not essential. Time series datasets are typically used in situations in which measurements, once made, are not revised or updated, but rather, where the mass of measurements accumulates, with new data added for each parameter being measured at each new time point. These characteristics of time series limit the demands we put on the technology we use to store time series and thus affect how we design that technology. Although some approaches for how best to store, access, and analyze this type of data are relatively new, the idea of time series data is actually quite an old one.

Time Series Data Is an Old Idea

It may surprise you to know that one of the great examples of the advantages to be reaped from collecting data as a time series—and doing it as a crowdsourced, open source, big data project—comes from the mid-19th century. The story starts with a sailor named Matthew Fontaine Maury, who came to be known as the Pathfinder of the Seas. When a leg injury forced him to quit ocean voyages in his thirties, he turned to scientific research in meteorology, astronomy, oceanography, and cartography, and a very extensive bit of whale watching, too.

Ship's captains and science officers had long been in the habit of keeping detailed logbooks during their voyages. Careful entries included the date and often the time of various measurements, such as how many knots the ship was traveling, calculations of latitude and longitude on specific days, and observations of ocean conditions, wildlife, weather, and more. A sample entry in a ship's log is shown in Figure 1-3.

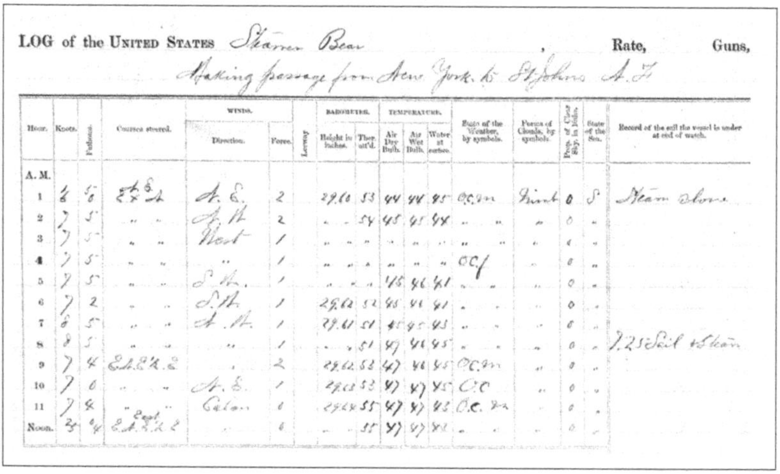

Figure 1-3. Old ship's log of the Steamship Bear as it steamed north as part of the 1884 Greely rescue mission to the arctic. Nautical logbooks are an early source of large-scale time series data.[1]

Maury saw the hidden value in these logs when analyzed collectively and wanted to bring that value to ships' captains. When Maury was put in charge of the US Navy's office known as the Depot of Charts and Instruments, he began a project to extract observations of winds and currents accumulated over many years in logbooks from many ships. He used this time series data to carry out an analysis that would enable him to recommend optimal shipping routes based on prevailing winds and currents.

---

1. From image digitized by http://www.oldweather.org and provided via http://www.naval-history.net. Image modified by Ellen Friedman and Ted Dunning.

In the winter of 1848, Maury sent one of his *Wind and Current Charts* to Captain Jackson, who commanded a ship based out of Baltimore, Maryland. Captain Jackson became the first person to try out the evidence-based route to Rio de Janeiro recommended by Maury's analysis. As a result, Captain Jackson was able to save 17 days on the outbound voyage compared to earlier sailing times of around 55 days, and even more on the return trip. When Jackson's ship returned more than a month early, news spread fast, and Maury's charts were quickly in great demand. The benefits to be gained from data mining of the painstakingly observed, recorded, and extracted time series data became obvious.

Maury's charts also played a role in setting a world record for the fastest sailing passage from New York to San Francisco by the clipper ship *Flying Cloud* in 1853, a record that lasted for over a hundred years. Of note and surprising at the time was the fact that the navigator on this voyage was a woman: Eleanor Creesy, the wife of the ship's captain and an expert in astronomy, ocean currents, weather, and data-driven decisions.

Where did crowdsourcing and open source come in? Not only did Maury use existing ship's logs, he encouraged the collection of more regular and systematic time series data by creating a template known as the "Abstract Log for the Use of American Navigators." The logbook entry shown in Figure 1-3 is an example of such an abstract log. Maury's abstract log included detailed data collection instructions and a form on which specific measurements could be recorded in a standardized way. The data to be recorded included date, latitude and longitude (at noon), currents, magnetic variation, and hourly measurements of ship's speed, course, temperature of air and water, and general wind direction, and any remarks considered to be potentially useful for other ocean navigators. Completing such abstract logs was the price a captain or navigator had to pay in order to receive Maury's charts.[2]

Time Series Data Sets Reveal Trends

One of the ways that time series data can be useful is to help recognize patterns or a trend. Knowing the value of a specific parameter at the current time is quite different than the ability to observe its behavior

---

2. *http://icoads.noaa.gov/maury.pdf*

over a long time interval. Take the example of measuring the concentration of some atmospheric component of interest. You may, for instance, be concerned about today's ozone level or the level for some particulate contaminant, especially if you have asthma or are planning an outdoor activity. In that case, just knowing the current day's value may be all you need in order to decide what precautions you want to take that day.

This situation is very different from what you can discover if you make many such measurements and record them as a function of the time they were made. Such a time series dataset makes it possible to discover dynamic patterns in the behavior of the condition in question as it changes over time. This type of discovery is what happened in a surprising way for a geochemical researcher named Charles David Keeling, starting in the mid-20th century.

David Keeling was a postdoc beginning a research project to study the balance between carbonate in the air, surface waters, and limestone when his attention was drawn to a very significant pattern in data he was collecting in Pasadena, California. He was using a very precise instrument to measure atmospheric CO_2 levels on different days. He found a lot of variation, mostly because of the influence of industrial exhaust in the area. So he moved to a less built–up location, the Big Sur region of the California coast near Monterrey, and repeated these measurements day and night. By observing atmospheric CO_2 levels as a function of time for a short time interval, he discovered a regular pattern of difference between day and night, with CO_2 levels higher at night.

This observation piqued Keeling's interest. He continued his measurements at a variety of locations and finally found funding to support a long-term project to measure CO_2 levels in the air at an altitude of 3,000 meters. He did this by setting up a measuring station at the top of the volcanic peak in Hawaii called Mauna Loa. As his time series for atmospheric CO_2 concentrations grew, he was able to discern another pattern of regular variation: seasonal changes. Keeling's data showed the CO_2 level was higher in the winter than the summer, which made sense given that there is more plant growth in the summer. But the most significant discovery was yet to come.

Keeling continued building his CO_2 time series dataset for many years, and the work has been carried on by others from the Scripps Institute of Oceanography and a much larger, separate observation being made by the US National Ocean and Atmospheric Administration (NOAA). The dataset includes measurements from 1958 to the present. Measured over half a century, this valuable scientific time series is the longest continuous measurement of atmospheric CO_2 levels ever made. As a result of collecting precise measurements as a function of time for so long, researchers have data that reveals a long-term and very disturbing trend: the levels of atmospheric CO_2 are increasing dramatically. From the time of Keeling's first observations to the present, CO_2 has increased from 313 ppm to over 400 ppm. That's an increase of 28% in just 56 years as compared to an increase of only 12% from 400,000 years ago to the start of the Keeling study (based on data from polar ice cores). Figure 1-4 shows a portion of the Keeling Curve and NOAA data.

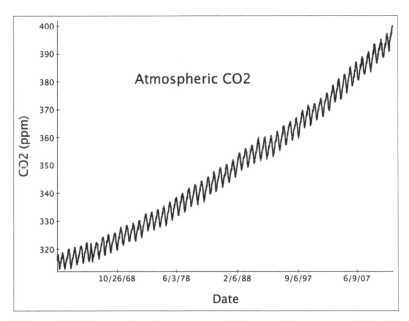

Figure 1-4. Time series data measured frequently over a sufficiently long time interval can reveal regular patterns of variation as well as long-term trends. This curve shows that the level of atmospheric CO_2 is steadily and significantly increasing. See the original data (http:// 1.usa.gov/1uKQFfd) from which this figure was drawn.

Not all time series datasets lead to such surprising and significant discoveries as did the CO_2 data, but time series are extremely useful in revealing interesting patterns and trends in data. Alternatively, a study of time series may show that the parameter being measured is either very steady or varies in very irregular ways. Either way, measurements made as a function of time make these behaviors apparent.

A New Look at Time Series Databases

These examples illustrate how valuable multiple observations made over time can be when stored and analyzed effectively. New methods are appearing for building time series databases that are able to handle very large datasets. For this reason, this book examines how large-scale time series data can best be collected, persisted, and accessed for analysis. It does not focus on methods for analyzing time series, although some of these methods were discussed in our previous book on anomaly detection. Nor is the book report intended as a comprehensive survey of the topic of time series data storage. Instead, we explore some of the fundamental issues connected with new types of time series databases (TSDB) and describe in general how you can use this type of data to advantage. We also give you tips that to make it easier to store and access time series data cost effectively and with excellent performance. Throughout, this book focuses on the practical aspects of time series databases.

Before we explore the details of how to build better time series databases, let's first look at several modern situations in which large-scale times series are useful.

CHAPTER 2

A New World for Time Series Databases

As we saw with the old ship's logs described in Chapter 1, time series data—tracking events or repeated measurements as a function of time—is an old idea, but one that's now an old idea in a new world. One big change is a much larger scale for traditional types of data. Differences in the way global business and transportation are done, as well as the appearance of new sources of data, have worked together to explode the volume of data being generated. It's not uncommon to have to deal with petabytes of data, even when carrying out traditional types of analysis and reporting. As a result, it has become harder to do the same things you used to do.

In addition to keeping up with traditional activities, you may also find yourself exposed to the lure of finding new insights through novel ways of doing data exploration and analytics, some of which need to use unstructured or semi-structured formats. One cause of the explosion in the availability of time series data is the widespread increase in reporting from sensors. You have no doubt heard the term Internet of Things (IoT), which refers to a proliferation of sensor data resulting in wide arrays of machines that report back to servers or communicate directly with each other. This mass of data offers great potential value if it is explored in clever ways.

How can you keep up with what you normally do and plus expand into new insights? Working with time series data is obviously less laborious today than it was for oceanographer Maury and his colleagues in the 19th century. It's astounding to think that they did by hand the painstaking work required to collect and analyze a daunting amount of data in order produce accurate charts for recommended shipping routes. Just having access to modern computers, however, isn't enough to solve the problems posed by today's world of time series data. Looking back 10 years, the amount of data that was once collected in 10 minutes for some very active systems is now generated every second. These new challenges need different tools and approaches.

The good news is that emerging solutions based on distributed computing technologies mean that now you can not only handle traditional tasks in spite of the onslaught of increasing levels of data, but you also can afford to expand the scale and scope of what you do. These innovative technologies include Apache Cassandra and a variety of distributions of Apache Hadoop. They share the desirable characteristic of being able to scale efficiently and of being able to use less-structured data than traditional database systems. Time series data could be stored as flat files, but if you will primarily want to access the data based on a time span, storing it as a time series database is likely a good choice. A TSDB is optimized for best performance for queries based on a range of time. New NoSQL approaches make use of non-relational databases with considerable advantages in flexibility and performance over traditional relational databases (RDBMS) for this purpose. See "NoSQL Versus RDBMS: What's the Difference, What's the Point?" for a general comparison of NoSQL databases with relational databases.

For the methods described in this book we recommend the Hadoop-based databases Apache HBase or MapR-DB. The latter is a non-relational database integrated directly into the file system of the MapR distribution derived from Apache Hadoop. The reason we focus on these Hadoop-based solutions is that they can not only execute rapid ingestion of time series data, but they also support rapid, efficient queries of time series databases. For the rest of this book, you should assume that whenever we say "time series database" without being more specific, we are referring to these NoSQL Hadoop-based database solutions augmented with technologies to make them work well with time series data.

NoSQL Versus RDBMS: What's the Difference, What's the Point?

NoSQL databases and relational databases share the same basic goals: to store and retrieve data and to coordinate changes. The difference is that NoSQL databases trade away some of the capabilities of relational databases in order to improve scalability. In particular, NoSQL databases typically have much simpler coordination capabilities than the transactions that traditional relational systems provide (or even none at all). The NoSQL databases usually eliminate all or most of SQL query language and, importantly, the complex optimizer required for SQL to be useful.

The benefits of making this trade include greater simplicity in the NoSQL database, the ability to handle semi-structured and denormalized data and, potentially, much higher scalability for the system. The drawbacks include a compensating increase in the complexity of the application and loss of the abstraction provided by the query optimizer. Losing the optimizer means that much of the optimization of queries has to be done inside the developer's head and is frozen into the application code. Of course, losing the optimizer also can be an advantage since it allows the developer to have much more predictable performance.

Over time, the originally hard-and-fast tradeoffs involving the loss of transactions and SQL in return for the performance and scalability of the NoSQL database have become much more nuanced. New forms of transactions are becoming available in some NoSQL databases that provide much weaker guarantees than the kinds of transactions in RDBMS. In addition, modern implementations of SQL such as open source Apache Drill allow analysts and developers working with NoSQL applications to have a full SQL language capability when they choose, while retaining scalability.

Until recently, the standard approach to dealing with large-scale time series data has been to decide from the start which data to sample, to study a few weeks' or months' worth of the sampled data, produce the desired reports, summarize some results to be archived, and then discard most or all of the original data. Now that's changing. There is a golden opportunity to do broader and deeper analytics, exploring data that would previously have been discarded. At modern rates of data production, even a few weeks or months is a large enough data volume that it starts to overwhelm traditional database methods. With the new scalable NoSQL platforms and tools for data storage and access, it's now feasible to archive years of raw or lightly processed data. These much finer-grained and longer histories are especially valuable in modeling needed for predictive analytics, for anomaly detection, for back-testing new models, and in finding long-term trends and correlations.

As a result of these new options, the number of situations in which data is being collected as time series is also expanding, as is the need for extremely reliable and high-performance time series databases (the subject of this book). Remember that it's not just a matter of asking yourself what data to save, but instead looking at *when saving data as a time series database is advantageous*. At very large scales, time-based queries can be implemented as large, contiguous scans that are very efficient if the data is stored appropriately in a time series database. And if the amount of data is very large, a non-relational TSDB in a NoSQL system is typically needed to provide sufficient scalability.

When considering whether to use these non-relational time series databases, remember the following considerations:

Use a non-relational TSDB when you:

- Have huge amount of data
- Mostly want to query based on time

The choice to use non-relational time series databases opens the door to discovery of patterns in time series data, long-term trends, and correlations between data representing different types of events. Before we move to Chapter 3, where we describe some key architectural concepts for building and accessing TSDBs, let's first look at some examples of *who uses time series data and why*?

Stock Trading and Time Series Data

Time series data has long been important in the financial sector. The exact timing of events is a critical factor in the transactions made by banks and stock exchanges. We don't have to look to the future to see very large data volumes in stock and commodity trading and the need for new solutions. Right now the extreme volume and rapid flow of data relating to bid and ask prices for stocks and commodities defines a new world for time series databases. Use cases from this sector make prime examples of the benefits of using non-relational time series databases.

What levels of data flow are we talking about? The Chicago Mercantile Exchange in the US has around 100 million live contracts and handles roughly 14 million contracts per day. This level of business results in an estimated 1.5 to 2 million messages per second. This level of volume and velocity potentially produces that many time series points as well. And there is an expected annual growth of around 33% in this market. Similarly, the New York Stock Exchange (NYSE) has over 4,000 stocks registered, but if you count related financial instruments, there are 1,000 times as many things to track. Each of these can have up to hundreds of quotes per second, and that's just at this one exchange. Think of the combined volume of sequential time-related trade data globally each day. To save the associated time series is a daunting task, but with modern technologies and techniques, such as those described in this book, to do so becomes feasible.

Trade data arrives so quickly that even very short time frames can show a lot of activity. Figure 2-1 visualizes the pattern of price and volume fluctuations of a single stock during just one minute of trading.

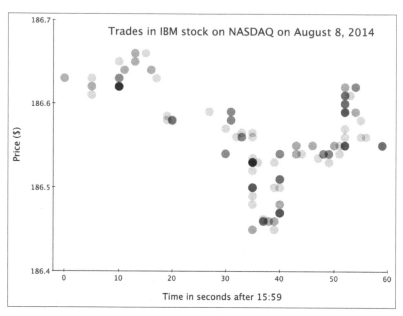

Figure 2-1. Data for the price of trades of IBM stock during the last minute of trading on one day of the NYSE. Each trade is marked with a semi-transparent dot. Darker dots represent multiple trades at the same time and price. This one stock traded more than once per second during this particular minute.

It may seem surprising to look at a very short time range in such detail, but with this high-frequency data, it is possible to see very short-term price fluctuations and to compare them to the behavior of other stocks or composite indexes. This fine-grained view becomes very important, especially in light of some computerized techniques in trading included broadly under the term "algorithmic trading." Processes such as algorithmic trading and high-frequency trading by institutions, hedge funds, and mutual funds can carry out large-volume trades in seconds without human intervention. The visualization in Figure 2-1 is limited to one-second resolution, but the programs handling trading for many hedge funds respond on a millisecond time scale. During any single second of trading, these programs can engage each other in an elaborate back-and-forth game of bluff and call as they make bids and offers.

Some such trades are triggered by changes in trading volumes over recent time intervals. Forms of program trading represent a sizable percentage of the total volume of modern exchanges. Computer-driven high-frequency trading is estimated to account for over 50% of all trades.

The velocity of trades and therefore the collection of trading data and the need in many cases for extremely small latency make the use of very high-performing time series databases extremely important. The time ranges of interest are extending in both directions. In addition to the very short time-range queries, long-term histories for time series data are needed, especially to discover complex trends or test strategies. Figure 2-2 shows the volume in millions of trades over a range of several years of activity at the NYSE and clearly reveals the unusual spike in volume during the financial crisis of late 2008 and 2009.

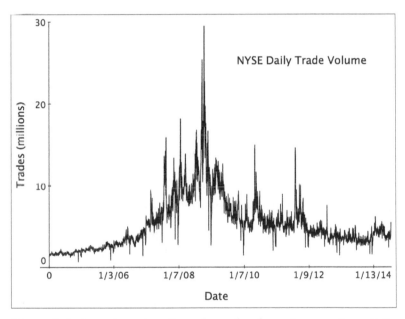

Figure 2-2. Long-term trends such as the sharp increase in activity leading up to and during the 2008–2009 economic crisis become apparent by visualizing the trade volume data for the New York Stock Exchange over a 10-year period.

Keeping long-term histories for trades of individual stocks and for total trading volume as a function of time is very different from the old-fashioned ticker tape reporting. A ticker tape did not record the absolute timing of trades, although the order of trades was preserved. It served as a moving current window of knowledge about a stock's price, but not as a long-term history of its behavior. In contrast, the long-term archives of trading data stored in modern TSDBs let you know exactly what happened and exactly when. This fine-grained view is important to meet government regulations for financial institutions and to be able to correlate trading behavior to other factors, including news events and sentiment analytics signals extracted from social media. These new kinds of inputs can be very valuable in predictive analytics.

Making Sense of Sensors

It's easy to see why the availability of new and affordable technologies to store, access, and analyze time series databases expands the possibilities in many sectors for measuring a wide variety of physical parameters. One of the fastest growing areas for generating large-scale time series data is in the use of sensors, both in familiar applications and in some new and somewhat surprising uses.

In Chapter 1 we considered the wide variety of sensor measurements collected on aircraft throughout a flight. Trucking is another area in which the use of time series data from sensors is expanding. Engine parameters, speed or acceleration, and location of the truck are among the variables being recorded as a function of time for each individual truck throughout its daily run. The data collected from these measurements can be used to address some very practical and profitable questions. For example, there are potentially very large tax savings when these data are analyzed to document actual road usage by each truck in a fleet. Trucking companies generally are required to pay taxes according to how much they drive on public roads. It's not just a matter of *how many* miles a truck drives; if it were, just using the record on the odometer would be sufficient. Instead, it's a matter of knowing *which* miles the truck drives—in other words, how much each truck is driven on the taxable roads. Trucks actually cover many miles off of these public roads, including moving through the large loading areas of supply warehouses or traveling through the roads that run through large landfills, in the case of waste-management vehicles.

If the trucking company is able to document their analysis of the position of each truck by time as well as to the location relative to specific roads, it's possible for the road taxes for each truck to be based on actual taxable road usage. Without this data and analysis, the taxes will be based on odometer readings, which may be much higher. Being able to accurately monitor overall engine performance is also a key economic issue in areas like Europe where vehicles may be subject to a carbon tax that varies in different jurisdictions. Without accurate records of location and engine operation, companies have to pay fees based on how much carbon they *may* have emitted instead of how much they actually did emit.

It's not just trucking companies who have gotten "smart" in terms of sensor measurements. Logistics are an important aspect of running a successful retail business, so knowing exactly what is happening to each pallet of goods at different points in time is useful for tracking goods, scheduling deliveries, and monitoring warehouse status. A smart pallet can be a source of time series data that might record events of interest such as when the pallet was filled with goods, when it was loaded or unloaded from a truck, when it was transferred into storage in a warehouse, or even the environmental parameters involved, such as temperature.

Similarly, it would be possible to equip commercial waste containers, called dumpsters in the US, with sensors to report on how full they are at different points in time. Why not just peek into the dumpster to see if it needs to be emptied? That might be sufficient if it's just a case of following the life of one dumpster, but waste-management companies in large cities must consider what is happening with hundreds of thousands of dumpsters. For shared housing such as apartments or condominiums, some cities recommend providing one dumpster for every four families, and there are dumpsters at commercial establishments such as restaurants, service stations, and shops. Periodically, the number of dumpsters at particular locations changes, such as in the case of construction sites. Seasonal fluctuations occur for both residential and commercial waste containers—think of the extra levels of trash after holidays for example.

Keeping a history of the rate of fill for individual dumpsters (a time series) can be useful in scheduling pickup routes for the large waste-management trucks that empty dumpsters. This level of management not only could improve customer service, but it also could result in fuel savings by optimizing the pattern for truck operations.

Manufacturing is another sector in which time series data from sensor measurements is extremely valuable. Quality control is a matter of constant concern in manufacturing as much today as it was in the past.

"Uncontrolled variation is the enemy of quality."

— Attributed to Edward Deming—engineer and management guru
in the late 20th century

In the quest for controlling variation, it's a natural fit to take advantage of new capabilities to collect many sensor measurements from the equipment used in manufacturing and store them in a time series database. The exact range of movement for a mechanical arm, the temperature of an extrusion tip for a polymer flow, vibrations in an engine —the variety of measurements is very broad in this use case. One of the many goals for saving this data as a time series is to be able to correlate conditions precisely to the quality of the product being made at specific points in time.

Talking to Towers: Time Series and Telecom

Mobile cell phone usage is now ubiquitous globally, and usage levels are increasing. In many parts of the world, for example, there's a growing dependency on mobile phones for financial transactions that take place constantly. While overall usage is increasing, there are big variations in the traffic loads on networks depending on residential population densities at different times of the day, on temporary crowds, and on special events that encourage phone use. Some of these special events are scheduled, such as the individual matches during the World Cup competition. Other special events that result in a spike in cell phone usage are not scheduled. These include earthquakes and fires or sudden political upheavals. Life events happen, and people use their phones to investigate or comment on them.

All of these situations that mean an increase in business are great news for telecommunication companies, but they also present some huge challenges in maintaining good customer service through reliable performance of the mobile networks. When in use, each mobile phone is constantly "talking" to the nearest cell phone tower, sending and receiving data. Now multiply that level of data exchange by the millions of phones in use, and you begin to see the size of the problem. Monitoring the data rates to and from cell towers is important in being able to recognize what constitutes a normal pattern of usage versus unusual fluctuations that could impair quality of service for some customers trying to share a tower. A situation that could cause this type of surge in cell phone traffic is shown in the illustration in Figure 2-3. A temporary influx of extra cell phone usage at key points during a sports event could overwhelm a network and cause poor connectivity for regular residential or commercial customers in the neighborhood. To accommodate this short-term swell in traffic, the telecom provider may be able to activate mini-towers installed near the stadium to handle the extra load. This activation can take time, and it is likely not cost-effective to use these micro-towers at low-traffic loads. Careful monitoring of the moment-to-moment patterns of usage is the basis for developing adaptive systems that respond appropriately to changes.

In order to monitor usage patterns, consider the traffic for each small geographical region nearby to a cell tower to be a separate time series. There are strong correlations between different time series during normal operation and specific patterns of correlation that arise during these flash crowd events that can be used to provide early warning. Not surprisingly, this analysis requires some pretty heavy time series lifting.

Figure 2-3. Time series databases provide an important tool in managing cell tower resources to provide consistent service for mobile phone customers despite shifting loads, such as those caused by a stadium full of people excitedly tweeting in response to a key play. Service to other customers in the area could be impaired if the large tower in this illustration is overwhelmed. When needed, auxiliary towers can be activated to accommodate the extra traffic.

Similarly, public utilities now use smart meters to report frequent measurements of energy usage at specific locations. These time series datasets can help the utility companies not only with billing, such as monitoring peak time of day usage levels, but also to redirect energy delivery relative to fluctuations in need or in response to energy generation by private solar arrays at residences or businesses. Water supply companies can also use detailed measurements of flow and pressure as a function of time to better manage their resources and customer experience.

Data Center Monitoring

Modern data centers are complex systems with a variety of operations and analytics taking place around the clock. Multiple teams need access at the same time, which requires coordination. In order to optimize resource use and manage workloads, system administrators monitor a huge number of parameters with frequent measurements for a fine-grained view. For example, data on CPU usage, memory residency, IO activity, levels of disk storage, and many other parameters are all useful to collect as time series.

Once these datasets are recorded as time series, data center operations teams can reconstruct the circumstances that lead to outages, plan upgrades by looking at trends, or even detect many kinds of security intrusion by noticing changes in the volume and patterns of data transfer between servers and the outside world.

Environmental Monitoring: Satellites, Robots, and More

The historic time series dataset for measurements of atmospheric CO_2 concentrations described in Chapter 1 is just one part of the very large field of environmental monitoring that makes use of time series data. Not only do the CO_2 studies continue, but similar types of long-term observations are used in various studies of meteorology and atmospheric conditions, in oceanography, and in monitoring seismic changes on land and under the ocean. Remote sensors from satellites collect huge amounts of data globally related to atmospheric humidity, wind direction, ocean currents, and temperatures, ozone concentrations in the atmosphere, and more. Satellite sensors can help scientists determine the amounts of photosynthesis taking place in the upper waters of the oceans by measuring concentrations of the light-collecting pigments such as chlorophyll.

For ocean conditions, additional readings are made from ships and from new technologies such as ocean-going robots. For example, the company Liquid Robotics headquartered in Sunnyvale, California, makes ocean-going robots known as wave gliders. There are several models, but the wave glider is basically an unmanned platform that carries a wide variety of equipment for measuring various ocean conditions. The ocean data collectors are powered by solar panels on the wave gliders, but the wave gliders themselves are propelled by wave energy. These self-propelled robotic sensors are not much bigger than a surfboard, and yet they have been able to travel from San Francisco to Hawaii and on to Japan and Australia, making measurements all along the way. They have even survived tropical storms and shark attacks. The amount of data they collect is staggering, and more and more of them are being launched.

Another new company involved in environmental monitoring also headquartered in Sunnyvale is Planet OS. They are a data aggregation company that uses data from satellites, in-situ instruments, HF radar, sonar, and more. Their sophisticated data handling includes very complicated time series databases related to a wide range of sensor data. These examples are just a few among the many projects involved in collecting environmental data to build highly detailed, global, long-term views of our planet.

The Questions to Be Asked

The time series data use cases described in this chapter just touch on a few key areas in which time series databases are important solutions. The best description of where time series data is of use is *practically everywhere measurements are made*. Thanks to new technologies to store and access large-scale time series data in a cost-effective way, time series data is becoming ubiquitous. The volume of data from use cases in which time series data has traditionally been important is expanding, and as people learn about the new tools available to handle data at scale, they are also considering the value of collecting data as a function of time in new situations as well.

With these changes in mind, it's helpful to step back and look in a more general way at some of the types of questions being addressed effectively by time series data. Here's a short list of some of the categories:

1. What are the short- and long-term trends for some measurement or ensemble of measurements? (prognostication)

2. How do several measurements correlate over a period of time? (introspection)

3. How do I build a machine-learning model based on the temporal behavior of many measurements correlated to externally known facts? (prediction)

4. Have similar patterns of measurements preceded similar events? (introspection)

5. What measurements might indicate the cause of some event, such as a failure? (diagnosis)

Now that you have an idea of some of the ways in which people are using large-scale time series data, we will turn to the details of how best to store and access it.

CHAPTER 3

Storing and Processing
Time Series Data

As we mentioned in previous chapters, a time series is a sequence of values, each with a time value indicating when the value was recorded. Time series data entries are rarely amended, and time series data is often retrieved by reading a contiguous sequence of samples, possibly after summarizing or aggregating the retrieved samples as they are retrieved. A time series database is a way to store multiple time series such that queries to retrieve data from one or a few time series for a particular time range are particularly efficient. As such, applications for which time range queries predominate are often good candidates for implementation using a time series database. As previously explained, the main topic of this book is the storage and processing of large-scale time series data, and for this purpose, the preferred technologies are NoSQL non-relational databases such as Apache HBase or MapR-DB.

Pragmatic advice for practical implementations of large-scale time series databases is the goal of this book, so we need to focus in on some basic steps that simplify and strengthen the process for real-world applications. We will look briefly at approaches that may be useful for small or medium-sized datasets and then delve more deeply into our main concern: how to implement large-scale TSDBs.

To get to a solid implementation, there are a number of design decisions to make. The drivers for these decisions are the parameters that define the data. How many distinct time series are there? What kind of data is being acquired? At what rate is the data being acquired? For how long must the data be kept? The answers to these questions help determine the best implementation strategy.

Roadmap to Key Ideas in This Chapter

Although we've already mentioned some central aspects to handling time series data, the current chapter goes into the most important ideas underlying methods to store and access time series in more detail and more deeply than previously. Chapter 4 then provides tips for how best to implement these concepts using existing open source software. There's a lot to absorb in these two chapters. So that you can better keep in mind how the key ideas fit together without getting lost in the details, here's a brief roadmap of this chapter:

- Flat files
  - Limited utility for time series; data will outgrow them, and access is inefficient
- True database: relational (RDBMS)
  - Will not scale well; familiar star schema inappropriate
- True database: NoSQL non-relational database
  - Preferred because it scales well; efficient and rapid queries based on time range
  - Basic design
    - Unique row keys with time series IDs; column is a time offset
    - Stores more than one time series
  - Design choices
    - Wide table stores data point-by-point
    - Hybrid design mixes wide table and blob styles
    - Direct blob insertion from memory cache

Now that we've walked through the main ideas, let's revisit them in some detail to explain their significance.

Simplest Data Store: Flat Files

You can extend this very simple design a bit to something slightly more advanced by using a more clever file format, such as the columnar file format Parquet, for organization. Parquet is an effective and simple, modern format that can store the time and a number of optional values. Figure 3-1 shows two possible Parquet schemas for recording time series. The schema on the left is suitable for special-purpose storage of time series data where you know what measurements are plausible. In the example on the left, only the four time series that are explicitly shown can be stored (tempIn, pressureIn, tempOut, pressureOut). Adding another time series would require changing the schema. The more abstract Parquet schema on the right in Figure 3-1 is much better for cases where you may want to embed more metadata about the time series into the data file itself. Also, there is no *a priori* limit on the number or names of different time series that can be stored in this format. The format on the right would be much more appropriate if you were building a time series library for use by other people.

```
message simpleSeries {              message fancySeries {
  repeated group sample {             repeated group block {
    required float t;                   repeated group tags {
    optional float tempIn;                optional string name;
    optional float pressureIn;            optional string value;
    optional float tempOut;             }
    optional float pressureOut;         repeated float time;
  }                                     repeated float value;
}                                     }
                                    }
```

Figure 3-1. Two possible schemas for storing time series data in Parquet. The schema on the left embeds knowledge about the problem domain in the names of values. Only the four time series shown can be stored without changing the schema. In contrast, the schema on the right is more flexible; you could add additional time series. It is also a bit more abstract, grouping many samples for a single time series into a single block.

Such a simple implementation of a time series—especially if you use a file format like Parquet—can be remarkably serviceable as long as the number of time series being analyzed is relatively small and as long as the time ranges of interest are large with respect to the partitioning time for the flat files holding the data.

While it is fairly common for systems to start out with a flat file implementation, it is also common for the system to outgrow such a simple implementation before long. The basic problem is that as the number of time series in a single file increases, the fraction of usable data for any particular query decreases, because most of the data being read belongs to other time series.

Likewise, when the partition time is long with respect to the average query, the fraction of usable data decreases again since most of the data in a file is outside the time range of interest. Efforts to remedy these problems typically lead to other problems. Using lots of files to keep the number of series per file small multiplies the number of files. Likewise, shortening the partition time will multiply the number of files as well. When storing data on a system such as Apache Hadoop using HDFS, having a large number of files can cause serious stability problems. Advanced Hadoop-based systems like MapR can easily handle the number of files involved, but retrieving and managing large numbers of very small files can be inefficient due to the increased seek time required.

To avoid these problems, a natural step is to move to some form of a real database to store the data. The best way to do this is not entirely obvious, however, as you have several choices about the type of database and its design. We will examine the issues to help you decide.

Moving Up to a Real Database: But Will RDBMS Suffice?

Even well-partitioned flat files will fail you in handling your large-scale time series data, so you will want to consider some type of true database. When first storing time series data in a database, it is tempting to use a so-called star schema design and to store the data in a relational database (RDBMS). In such a database design, the core data is stored in a fact table that looks something like what is shown in Figure 3-2.

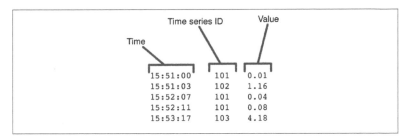

Figure 3-2. A fact table design for a time series to be stored in a relational database. The time, a series ID, and a value are stored. Details of the series are stored in a dimension table.

In a star schema, one table stores most of the data with references to other tables known as dimensions. A core design assumption is that the dimension tables are relatively small and unchanging. In the time series fact table shown in Figure 3-2, the only dimension being referenced is the one that gives the details about the time series themselves, including what measured the value being stored. For instance, if our time series is coming from a factory with pumps and other equipment, we might expect that several values would be measured on each pump such as inlet and outlet pressures and temperatures, pump vibration in different frequency bands, and pump temperature. Each of these measurements for each pump would constitute a separate time series, and each time series would have information such as the pump serial number, location, brand, model number, and so on stored in a dimension table.

A star schema design like this is actually used to store time series in some applications. We can also use a design like this in most NoSQL databases as well. A star schema addresses the problem of having lots of different time series and can work reasonably well up to levels of hundreds of millions or billions of data points. As we saw in Chapter 1, however, even 19th century shipping data produced roughly a billion data points. As of 2014, the NASDAQ stock exchange handles a billion trades in just over three months. Recording the operating conditions on a moderate-sized cluster of computers can produce half a billion data points in a day.

Moreover, simply storing the data is one thing; retrieving it and processing it is quite another. Modern applications such as machine learning systems or even status displays may need to retrieve and process as many as a million data points in a second or more.

While relational systems can scale into the lower end of these size and speed ranges, the costs and complexity involved grows very fast. As data scales continue to grow, a larger and larger percentage of time series applications just don't fit very well into relational databases. Using the star schema but changing to a NoSQL database doesn't particularly help, either, because the core of the problem is in the use of a star schema in the first place, not just the amount of data.

NoSQL Database with Wide Tables

The core problem with the star schema approach is that it uses one row per measurement. One technique for increasing the rate at which data can be retrieved from a time series database is to store many values in each row. With some NoSQL databases such as Apache HBase or MapR-DB, the number of columns in a database is nearly unbounded as long as the number of columns with active data in any particular row is kept to a few hundred thousand. This capability can be exploited to store multiple values per row. Doing this allows data points to be retrieved at a higher speed because the maximum rate at which data can be scanned is partially dependent on the number of rows scanned, partially on the total number of values retrieved, and partially on the total volume of data retrieved. By decreasing the number of rows, that part of the retrieval overhead is substantially cut down, and retrieval rate is increased. Figure 3-3 shows one way of using wide tables to decrease the number of rows used to store time series data. This technique is similar to the default table structure used in OpenTSDB, an open source database that will be described in more detail in Chapter 4. Note that such a table design is very different from one that you might expect to use in a system that requires a detailed schema be defined ahead of time. For one thing, the number of possible columns is absurdly large if you need to actually write down the schema.

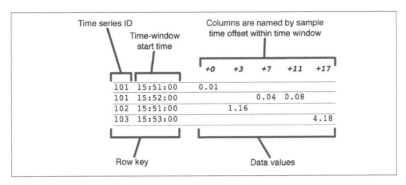

Figure 3-3. Use of a wide table for NoSQL time series data. The key structure is illustrative; in real applications, a binary format might be used, but the ordering properties would be the same.

Because both HBase and MapR-DB store data ordered by the primary key, the key design shown in Figure 3-3 will cause rows containing data from a single time series to wind up near one another on disk. This design means that retrieving data from a particular time series for a time range will involve largely sequential disk operations and therefore will be much faster than would be the case if the rows were widely scattered. In order to gain the performance benefits of this table structure, the number of samples in each time window should be substantial enough to cause a significant decrease in the number of rows that need to be retrieved. Typically, the time window is adjusted so that 100–1,000 samples are in each row.

NoSQL Database with Hybrid Design

The table design shown in Figure 3-3 can be improved by collapsing all of the data for a row into a single data structure known as a blob. This blob can be highly compressed so that less data needs to be read from disk. Also, if HBase is used to store the time series, having a single column per row decreases the per-column overhead incurred by the on-disk format that HBase uses, which further increases performance. The hybrid-style table structure is shown in Figure 3-4, where some rows have been collapsed using blob structures and some have not.

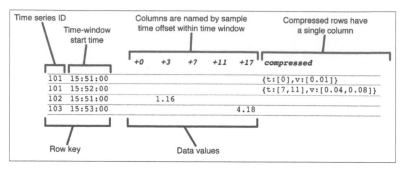

Figure 3-4. In the hybrid design, rows can be stored as a single data structure (blob). Note that the actual compressed data would likely be in a binary, compressed format. The compressed data are shown here in JSON format for ease of understanding.

Data in the wide table format shown in Figure 3-3 can be progressively converted to the compressed format (blob style) shown in Figure 3-4 as soon as it is known that little or no new data is likely to arrive for that time series and time window. Commonly, once the time window ends, new data will only arrive for a few more seconds, and the compression of the data can begin. Since compressed and uncompressed data can coexist in the same row, if a few samples arrive after the row is compressed, the row can simply be compressed again to merge the blob and the late-arriving samples.

The conceptual data flow for this hybrid-style time series database system is shown in Figure 3-5.

Converting older data to blob format in the background allows a substantial increase in the rate at which the renderer depicted in Figure 3-5 can retrieve data for presentation. On a 4-node MapR cluster, for instance, 30 million data points can be retrieved, aggregated and plotted in about 20 seconds when data is in the compressed form.

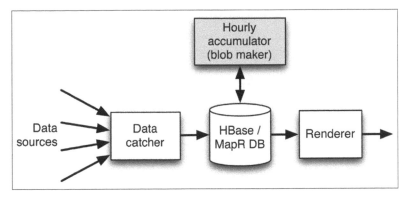

Figure 3-5. Data flow for the hybrid style of time series database. Data arrives at the catcher from the sources and is inserted into the NoSQL database. In the background, the blob maker rewrites the data later in compressed blob form. Data is retrieved and reformatted by the renderer.

Going One Step Further: The Direct Blob Insertion Design

Compression of old data still leaves one performance bottleneck in place. Since data is inserted in the uncompressed format, the arrival of each data point requires a row update operation to insert the value into the database. This row update can limit the insertion rate for data to as little as 20,000 data points per second per node in the cluster.

On the other hand, the direct blob insertion data flow diagrammed in Figure 3-6 allows the insertion rate to be increased by as much as roughly 1,000-fold. How does the direct blob approach get this bump in performance? The essential difference is that the blob maker has been moved into the data flow between the catcher and the NoSQL time series database. This way, the blob maker can use incoming data from a memory cache rather than extracting its input from wide table rows already stored in the storage tier.

The basic idea is that data is kept in memory as samples arrive. These samples are also written to log files. These log files are the "restart logs" shown in Figure 3-6 and are flat files that are stored on the Hadoop system but not as part of the storage tier itself. The restart logs allow the in-memory cache to be repopulated if the data ingestion pipeline has to be restarted.

In normal operations, at the end of a time window, new in-memory structures are created, and the now static old in-memory structures are used to create compressed data blobs to write to the database. Once the data blobs have been written, the log files are discarded. Compare the point in the data flow at which writes occur in the two scenarios. In the hybrid approach shown in Figure 3-5, the entire incoming data stream is written point-by-point to the storage tier, then read again by the blob maker. Reads are approximately equal to writes. Once data is compressed to blobs, it is again written to the database. In contrast, in the main data flow of the direct blob insertion approach shown in Figure 3-6, the full data stream is only written to the memory cache, which is fast, rather than to the database. Data is not written to the storage tier until it's compressed into blobs, so writing can be much faster. The number of database operations is decreased by the average number of data points in each of the compressed data blobs. This decrease can easily be a factor in the thousands.

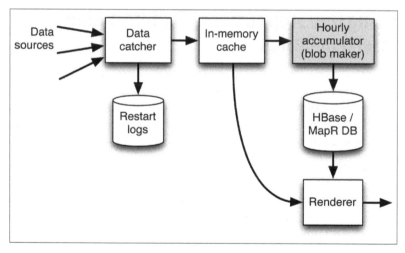

Figure 3-6. Data flow for the direct blob insertion approach. The catcher stores data in the cache and writes it to the restart logs. The blob maker periodically reads from the cache and directly inserts compressed blobs into the database. The performance advantage of this design comes at the cost of requiring access by the renderer to data buffered in the cache as well as to data already stored in the time series database.

What are the advantages of this direct blobbing approach? A real-world example shows what it can do. This architecture has been used to insert in excess of 100 million data points per second into a MapR-DB table using just 4 active nodes in a 10-node MapR cluster. These nodes are fairly high-performance nodes, with 16 cores, lots of RAM, and 12 well-configured disk drives per node, but you should be able to achieve performance within a factor of 2–5 of this level using most hardware.

This level of performance sounds like a lot of data, possibly more than most of us would need to handle, but in Chapter 5 we will show why ingest rates on that level can be very useful even for relatively modest applications.

Why Relational Databases Aren't Quite Right

At this point, it is fair to ask why a relational database couldn't handle nearly the same ingest and analysis load as is possible by using a hybrid schema with MapR-DB or HBase. This question is of particular interest when only blob data is inserted and no wide table data is used, because modern relational databases often have blob or array types.

The answer to this question is that a relational database running this way will provide reasonable, but not stellar, ingestion and retrieval rates. The real problem with using a relational database for a system like this is not performance, per se. Instead, the problem is that by moving to a blob style of data storage, you are giving up almost all of the virtues of a relational system. Additionally, SQL doesn't provide a good abstraction method to hide the details of accessing of a blob-based storage format. SQL also won't be able to process the data in any reasonable way, and special features like multirow transactions won't be used at all. Transactions, in particular, are a problem here because even though they wouldn't be used, this feature remains, at a cost. The requirement that a relational database support multirow transactions makes these databases much more difficult to scale to multinode configurations. Even getting really high performance out of a single node can require using a high-cost system like Oracle. With a NoSQL system like Apache HBase or MapR-DB instead, you can simply add additional hardware to get more performance.

This pattern of paying a penalty for unused features that get in the way of scaling a system happens in a number of high-performance systems. It is common that the measures that must be taken to scale a system inherently negate the virtues of a conventional relational database, and if you attempt to apply them to a relational database, you still do not get the scaling you desire. In such cases, moving to an alternative database like HBase or MapR-DB can have substantial benefits because you gain both performance and scalability.

Hybrid Design: Where Can I Get One?

These hybrid wide/blob table designs can be very alluring. Their promise of enormous performance levels is exciting, and the possibility that they can run on fault-tolerant, Hadoop-based systems such as the MapR distribution make them attractive from an operational point of view as well. These new approaches are not speculation; they have been built and they do provide stunning results. The description we've presented here so far, however, is largely conceptual. What about real implementations? The next chapter addresses exactly how you can realize these new designs by describing how you can use OpenTSDB, an open source time series database tool, along with special open source MapR extensions. The result is a practical implementation able to take advantage of the concepts described in this chapter to achieve high performance with a large-scale time series database as is needed for modern use cases.

CHAPTER 4

Practical Time Series Tools

"In theory, theory and practice are the same. In practice, they are not."

—Albert Einstein

As valuable as theory is, practice matters more. Chapter 3 described the theory behind high-performance time series databases leading up to the hybrid and direct-insertion blob architecture that allows very high ingest and analysis rates. This chapter describes how that theory can be implemented using open source software. The open source tools described in this chapter mainly comprise those listed in Table 4-1.

Table 4-1. Open source tools useful for preparing, loading, and accessing data in high-performance NoSQL time series databases.

Open Source Tool	Author	Purpose
Open TSDB	Benoit Sigoure (originally)	Collect, process, and load time series data into storage tier
Extensions to Open TSDB	MapR Technologies	Enable direct blog insertion
Grafana	Torkel Ödegaard and Coding Instinct AB	User interface for accessing and visualizing time series data

We also show how to analyze Open TSDB time series data using open source tools such as R and Apache Spark. At the end of this chapter, we describe how you can attach Grafana, an open source dashboarding tool, to Open TSDB to make it much more useful.

Introduction to Open TSDB: Benefits and Limitations

Originally just for systems monitoring, Open TSDB has proved far more versatile and useful than might have been imagined originally. Part of this versatility and longevity is due to the fact that the underlying storage engine, based on either Apache HBase or MapR-DB, allows a high degree of schema flexibility. The Open TSDB developers have used this to their advantage by starting with something like a star schema design, moving almost immediately to a wide table design, and later extending it with a compressor function to convert wide rows into blobs. (The concepts behind these approaches was explained in Chapter 3.) As the blob architecture was introduced, the default time window was increased from the original 60 seconds to a more blob-friendly one hour in length.

As it stands, however, Open TSDB also suffers a bit from its history and will not support extremely high data rates. This limitation is largely caused by the fact that data is only compacted into the performance-friendly blob format after it has already been inserted into the database in the performance-unfriendly wide table format.

The default user interface of Open TSDB is also not suitable for most users, especially those whose expectations have been raised by commercial quality dashboarding and reporting products. Happily, the open source Grafana project described later in this chapter now provides a user interface with a much higher level of polish. Notably, Grafana can display data from, among other things, an Open TSDB instance.

Overall, Open TSDB plus HBase or MapR-DB make an interesting core storage engine. Adding on Grafana gives users the necessary user interface with a bit of sizzle. All that is further needed to bring the system up to top performance is to add a high-speed turbo-mode data ingestion framework and the ability to script analyses of data stored in the database. We also show how to do both of these things in this chapter.

We focus on Open TSDB in this chapter because it has an internal data architecture that supports very high-performance data recording. If you don't need high data rates, the InfluxDB project may be a good alternative for your needs. InfluxDB provides a very nice query language, the ability to have standing queries, and a nice out-of-the-box interface. Grafana can interface with either Influx DB or Open TSDB. Let's take a look in more detail about how native Open TSDB works before introducing the high-performance, direct blob extensions contributed by MapR.

Architecture of Open TSDB

In Chapter 3 we described the options to build a time series database with a wide table design based on loading data point by point or by pulling data from the table and using a background blob maker to compress data and reload blobs to the storage tier, resulting in hybrid style tables (wide row + blob). These two options are what basic Open TSDB provides. The architecture of Open TSDB is shown in Figure 4-1. This figure is taken with minor modifications from the Open TSDB documentation.

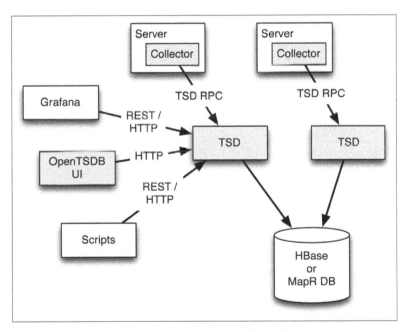

Figure 4-1. Open TSDB consists of a number of cooperating compo-
nents to load and access data from the storage tier of a time series da-
tabase. These include data collectors, time-series daemons (TSD), and
various user interface functions. Open TSDB components are colored
gray.

On servers where measurements are made, there is a collector process that sends data to the time series daemon (TSD) using the TSD RPC protocol. The time series daemons are responsible for looking up the time series to which the data is being appended and inserting each data point as it is received into the storage tier. A secondary thread in the TSD later replaces old rows with blob-formatted versions in a process known as row compaction. Because the TSD stores data into the storage tier immediately and doesn't keep any important state in memory, you can run multiple TSD processes without worrying about them stepping on each other. The TSD architecture shown here corresponds to the data flow depicted in the previous chapter in Figure 3-5 to produce hybrid-style tables. Note that the data catcher and the background blob maker of that figure are contained within the TSD component shown here in Figure 4-1.

User interface components such as the original Open TSDB user interface communicate directly with the TSD to retrieve data. The TSD retrieves the requested data from the storage tier, summarizes and aggregates it as requested, and returns the result. In the native Open TSDB user interface, the data is returned directly to the user's browser in the form of a PNG plot generated by the Gnuplot program. External interfaces and analysis scripts can use the PNG interface, but they more commonly use the REST interface of Open TSDB to read aggregated data in JSON form and generate their own visualizations.

Open TSDB suffers a bit in terms of ingestion performance by having collectors to send just a few data points at a time (typically just one point at a time) and by inserting data in the wide table format before later reformatting the data into blob format (this is the standard hybrid table data flow). Typically, it is unusual to be able to insert data into the wide table format at higher than about 10,000 data points per second per storage tier node. Getting ingestion rates up to or above a million data points per second therefore requires a large number of nodes in the storage tier. Wanting faster ingestion is not just a matter of better performance always being attractive; many modern situations produce data at such volume and velocity that in order be able to store and analyze it as a time series, it's necessary to increase the data load rates for the time series database in order to the do the projects at all.

This limitation on bulk ingestion speed can be massively improved by using an alternative ingestion program to directly write data into the storage tier in blob format. We will describe how this works in the next section.

Value Added: Direct Blob Loading for High Performance

An alternative to inserting each data point one by one is to buffer data in memory and insert a blob containing the entire batch. The trick is to move the blob maker upstream of insertion into the storage tier as described in Chapter 3 and Figure 3-6. The first time the data hits the table, it is already compressed as a blob. Inserting entire blobs of data this way will help if the time windows can be sized so that a large number of data points are included in each blob. Grouping data like this improves ingestion performance because the number of rows that need to be written to the storage tier is decreased by a factor equal to the average number of points in each blob. The total number of bytes may also be decreased if you compress the data being inserted. If you can arrange to have 1,000 data points or more per blob, ingest rates can be very high. As mentioned in Chapter 3, in one test with one data point per second and one-hour time windows, ingestion into a 4-node storage tier in a 10-node MapR cluster exceeded 100 million data points per second. This rate is more than 1,000 times faster than the system was able to ingest data without direct blob insertion.

To accomplish this high-performance style of data insertion with live data arriving at high velocity as opposed to historical data, it is necessary to augment the native Open TSDB with capabilities such as those provided by the open source extensions developed by MapR and described in more detail in the following section. Figure 4-2 gives us a look inside the modified time series daemon (TSD) as modified for direct blob insertion. These open source modifications will work on databases built with Apache HBase or with MapR-DB.

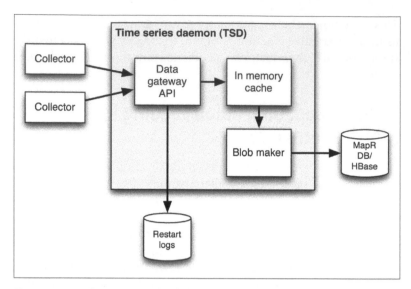

Figure 4-2. Changes inside the TSD when using extensions to Open TSDB that enable high-speed ingestion of rapid streaming data. Data is ingested initially to the storage tier in the blob-oriented format that stores many data points per row.

A New Twist: Rapid Loading of Historical Data

Using the extensions to Open TSDB, it is also possible to set up a separate data flow that loads data in blob-style format directly to the storage tier independently of the TSD. The separate blob loader is particularly useful with historical data for which there is no need to access recent data prior to its insertion into the storage tier. This design can be used at the same time as either a native or a modified TSD is in use for other data sources such as streaming data. The use of the separate blob loader for historical data is shown in Figure 4-3.

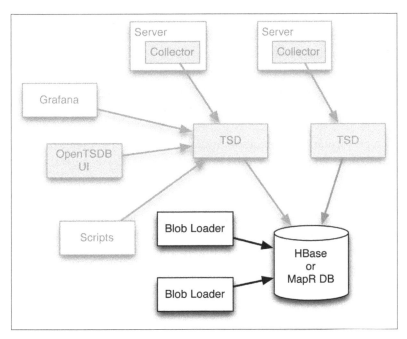

Figure 4-3. Historical data can be ingested at high speed through direct blob ingenstion by using the blob loader alongside Open TSDB, without needing an in-memory cache. Additional architectural components are shown grayed out here for context.

When using this blob loader, no changes are needed to the TSD systems or to the UI components since the blob loader is simply loading data in a format that Open TSDB already uses. In fact, you can be ingesting data in the normal fashion at the same time that you are loading historical data using the blob loader.

The blob loader accelerates data ingestion by short-circuiting the normal load path of Open TSDB. The effect is that data can be loaded at an enormous rate because the number of database operations is decreased by a large factor for data that has a sufficiently large number of samples in each time window.

Since unmodified Open TSDB can only retrieve data from the Apache HBase or MapR-DB storage tier, using the direct bulk loader of the extension means that any data buffered in the blob loader's memory and not yet written to the data tier cannot be seen by Open TSDB. This is fine for test or historical data, but is often not acceptable for live data ingestion. For test and historical ingestion, it is desirable to have much higher data rates than for production use, so it may be acceptable to use conventional ingestion for current data and use direct bulk only for other testing and backfill.

Summary of Open Source Extensions to Open TSDB for Direct Blob Loading

The performance acceleration available with open source MapR extensions to TSDB can be used in several ways. These general modes of using the extensions include:

Direct bulk loader
> The direct bulk loader loads data directly into storage tier in the Open TSDB blob format. This is the highest-performance load path and is suitable for loading historical data while the TSD is loading current data.

File loader
> The file loader loads files via the new TSD bulk API. Loading via the bulk API decreases performance somewhat but improves isolation between components since the file loader doesn't need to know about internal Open TSDB data formats.

TSD API for bulk loading
> This bulk load API is an entry point in the REST API exposed by the TSD component of Open TSDB. The bulk load API can be used in any collector instead of the point-by-point insertion API. The advantage of using the bulk API is that if the collector falls behind for any reason, it will be able to load many data points in each call to the API, which will help it catch up.

In-memory buffering for TSD
> The bulk load API is supported by in-memory buffering of data in the TSD. As data arrives, it is inserted into a buffer in the TSD. When a time window ends, the TSD will write the contents of the buffers into the storage tier in already blobbed format. Data buffered in memory is combined with data from the storage tier to satisfy any queries that require data from the time period that the buffer covers.

The current primary use of the direct bulk loader is to load large amounts of historical data in a short amount of time. Going forward, the direct bulk loader may be deprecated in favor of the file loader to isolate knowledge of the internal file formats.

The file loader has the advantage that it uses the REST API for bulk loading and therefore, data being loaded by the file loader will be visible by queries as it is loaded.

These enhancements to Open TSDB are available on github (*https://github.com/mapr-demos/opentsdb*). Over time, it is expected that they will be integrated into the upstream Open TSDB project.

Accessing Data with Open TSDB

Open TSDB has a built-in user interface, but it also allows direct access to time series data via a REST interface. In a few cases, the original data is useful, but most applications are better off with some sort of summary of the original data. This summary might have multiple data streams combined into one or it might have samples for a time period aggregated together. Open TSDB allows reduction of data in this fashion by allowing a fixed query structure.

In addition to data access, Open TSDB provides introspection capabilities that allow you to determine all of the time series that have data in the database and several other minor administrative capabilities.

The steps that Open TSDB performs to transform the raw data into the processed data it returns include:

Selection
> The time series that you want are selected from others by giving the metric name and some number of tag/value pairs.

Grouping
> The selected data can be grouped together. These groups determine the number of time series that are returned in the end. Grouping is optional.

Down-sampling
> It is common for the time series data retrieved by a query to have been sampled at a much higher rate than is desired for display. For instance, you might want to display a full year of data that was sampled every second. Display limitations mean that it is impossible to see anything more than about 1–10,000 data points. Open TSDB can downsample the retrieved data to match this limit. This makes plotting much faster as well.

Aggregation
Data for particular time windows are aggregated using any of a number of pre-specified functions such as average, sum, or minimum.

Interpolation
The time scale of the final results regularized at the end by interpolating as desired to particular standard intervals. This also ensures that all the data returned have samples at all of the same points.

Rate conversion
The last step is the optional conversion from counts to rates.

Each of these steps can be controlled via parameters in the URLs of the REST request that you need to send to the time series daemon (TSD) that is part of Open TSDB.

Working on a Higher Level

While you can use the REST interface directly to access data from Open TSDB, there are packages in a variety of languages that hide most of the details. Packages are available in R, Go, and Ruby for accessing data and more languages for pushing data into Open TSDB. A complete list of packages known to the Open TSDB developers can be found in the Open TSDB documentation in Appendix A.

As an example of how easy this can make access to Open TSDB data, here is a snippet of code in R that gets data from a set of metrics and plots them

```
result <- tsd_get(metric, start, tags=c(site="*"),
downsample="10m-avg")
library(zoo)
z <- with(result, zoo(value, timestamp))
filtered <- rollapply(z, width=7, FUN=median)
plot(merge(z, filtered))
```

This snippet is taken from the README for the github project (*https://github.com/holstius/opentsdbr*). The first line reads the data, grouping by site and downsampling to 10-minute intervals using an arithmetic average. The second line converts to a time series data type and computes a rolling median version of the data. The last line plots the data.

Using a library like this is an excellent way to get the benefits of the simple conceptual interface that Open TSDB provides combined with whatever your favorite language might be.

Using a package like this to access data stored in Open TSDB works relatively well for moderate volumes of data (up to a few hundred thousand data points, say), but it becomes increasingly sluggish as data volumes increase. Downsampling is a good approach to manage this, but downsampling discards information that you may need in your analysis. At some point, you may find that the amount of data that you are trying to retrieve from your database is simply too large either because downloading the data takes too long or because analysis in tools like R or Go becomes too slow.

If and when this happens, you will need to move to a more scalable analysis tool that can process the data in parallel.

Accessing Open TSDB Data Using SQL-on-Hadoop Tools

If you need to analyze large volumes of time series data beyond what works with the REST interface and downsampling, you probably also need to move to parallel execution of your analysis. At this point, it is usually best to access the contents of the Open TSDB data directly via the HBase API rather than depending on the REST interface that the TSD process provides.

You might expect to use SQL or the new SQL-on-Hadoop tools for this type of parallel access and analysis. Unfortunately, the wide table and blob formats that Open TSDB uses in order to get high performance can make it more difficult to access this data using SQL-based tools than you might expect. SQL as a language is not a great choice for actually analyzing time series data. When it comes to simply accessing data from Open TSDB, the usefulness of SQL depends strongly on which tool you select, as elaborated in the following sections. For some tools, the non-relational data formats used in Open TSDB can be difficult to access without substantial code development. In any case, special techniques that vary by tool are required to analyze time series data from Open TSDB. New SQL-on-Hadoop tools are being developed. In the next sections, we compare some of the currently available tools with regard to how well they let you access your time series database and Open TSDB.

Using Apache Spark SQL

Apache Spark SQL has some advantages in working with time series databases. Spark SQL is very different from Apache Hive in that it is embedded in and directly accessible from a full programming language. The first-class presence of Scala in Spark SQL programs makes it much easier to manipulate time series data from Open TSDB.

In particular, with Spark SQL, you can use an RDD (resilient distributed dataset) directly as an input, and that RDD can be populated by any convenient method. That means that you can use a range scan to read a number of rows from the Open TSDB data tier in either HBase or MapR-DB into memory in the form of an RDD. This leaves you with an RDD where the keys are row keys and the values are HBase Result structures. The `getFamilyMap` method can then be used to get all columns and cell values for that row. These, in turn, can be emitted as tuples that contain metric, timestamp, and value. The `flatmap` method is useful here because it allows each data row to be transformed into multiple time series samples.

You can then use any SQL query that you like directly on these tuples as stored in the resulting RDD. Because all processing after reading rows from HBase is done in memory and in parallel, the processing speed will likely be dominated by the cost of reading the rows of data from the data tier. Furthermore, in Spark, you aren't limited by language. If SQL isn't convenient, you can do any kind of Spark computation just as easily.

A particularly nice feature of using Spark to analyze metric data is that the framework already handles most of what you need to do in a fairly natural way. You need to write code to transform OpenTSDB rows into samples, but this is fairly straightforward compared to actually extending the platform by writing an input format or data storage module from scratch.

Why Not Apache Hive?

Analyzing time series data from OpenTSDB using Hive is much more difficult than it is with Spark. The core of the problem is that the HBase storage engine for Hive requires that data be stored using a very standard, predefined schema. With Open TSDB, the names of the columns actually contain the time portion of the data, and it isn't possible to write a fully defined schema to describe the tables. Not only are there a large number of possible columns (more than 10^{1000}), but the names of the columns are part of the data. Hive doesn't like that, so this fact has to be hidden from it.

The assumptions of Hive's design are baked in at a pretty basic level in the Hive storage engine, particularly with regard to the assumption that each column in the database represents a single column in the result. The only way to have Hive understand OpenTSDB is to clone and rewrite the entire HBase storage engine that is part of Hive. At that point, each row of data from the OpenTSDB table can be returned as an array of tuples containing one element for time and one for value. Each such row can be exploded using a lateral view join.

While it is possible to use Hive to analyze Open TSDB data, it is currently quite difficult. Spark is likely a better option.

Adding Grafana or Metrilyx for Nicer Dashboards

The default user interface for Open TSDB is very basic and not suitable for building embedded dashboards; it definitely is a bit too prickly for most ordinary users. In addition, the plots are produced using a tool called Gnuplot, whose default plot format looks very dated. A more convenient visualization interface is desirable.

One good solution is the open source dashboard editor known as Grafana. The Open TSDB REST API can provide access to data, and the team behind the Grafana project has used that access to build a high-quality data visualization interface for Open TSDB and other time series databases such as InfluxDB. A sample result is shown in Figure 4-4.

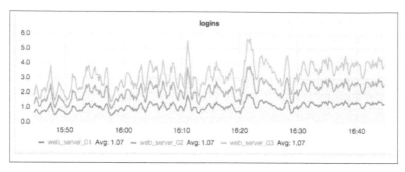

Figure 4-4. A sample plot from Grafana. This plot is taken from the sample instance that can be accessed from the project home page (http://grafana.org/).

Installation of Grafana is quite simple because it runs entirely on the client side using JavaScript. All you need to run Grafana is a web server that can serve static files such as Twistd or nginx. You will also have to make sure that your users' browsers can access the Open TSDB REST interface either directly or through a proxy. Using a proxy is a good idea if you want to ensure that users see data but can't modify it. If you want to allow users to define new dashboards, you will need to install and run an Elasticsearch instance as well. Grafana is available at *http:// grafana.org/*.

Another option for nicer dashboards with Open TSDB is Metrilyx, a package recently open sourced by Ticketmaster. Installing Metrilyx is a bit more involved than installing Grafana because there are additional dependencies (on nginx, Elasticsearch, Mongo and, optionally, Postgres), but there are some benefits such as the use of websockets in order to improve the responsiveness of the display. Keep in mind that while Metrilyx has been in use inside Ticketmaster for some time, it has only recently been released as open source. There may be some teething issues as a result due to the change in environment. Metrilyx is available at *https://github.com/Ticketmaster/metrilyx-2.0*.

Possible Future Extensions to Open TSDB

The bulk API extension to Open TSDB's REST interface assumes that data can be buffered in memory by the TSD. This violates the design assumptions of Open TSDB by making the TSD keep significant amounts of state information in memory. This has several negative effects, the most notable being that a failure of the TSD will likely cause data loss. Even just restarting a TSD process means that there is a short moment in time when there is no process to handle incoming data.

In the original Open TSDB design, this was never a problem because TSD processes are stateless by design. This means that you can run several such processes simultaneously and simply pick one at random to handle each API request. Each request that delivers data to the TSD will cause an immediate update of the storage tier, and all requests that ask the TSD are satisfied by reference to the database.

With in-memory buffering, the TSD is no longer stateless, and we therefore lose the benefits of that design. These issues do not affect the use of the bulk API for loading historical or test data because we can simply dedicate a TSD for bulk loading, restarting loading if the TSD fails or needs to be restarted. Similarly, the direct bulk loader is not affected by these considerations.

At this time, the in-memory caching that has been implemented in association with the bulk API has no provisions to allow restarts or multiple TSD processes. The next section describes one design that will support these capabilities safely.

Cache Coherency Through Restart Logs

Ultimately, it is likely to be desirable to allow multiple TSDs to be run at the same time and still use the in-memory caching for performance. This however, leads to a situation where new data points and requests for existing data could go to any TSD at all. In order to ensure that all TSDs have consistent views of all data, we need to have a cache coherency protocol where all new data accepted by any TSD has a very high likelihood of being present on every TSD very shortly after it arrives.

In order to do this simply, we require all TSDs to write restart logs that contain a record of all the transactions that they have received as well as a record of exactly when blobs are written to the storage tier. All TSDs can then read the restart logs of all of the other TSDs. This will help in two ways. First, all TSDs, including those recently started, will have very nearly identical memory states. Secondly, only one TSD will actually write each row to the database. Such a design avoids nearly all coordination at the cost of requiring that all recent data points be kept in multiple TSD memory spaces.

This design requires that a TSD be able to read restart logs and modify its in-memory representation at the full production data rate, possibly using several hardware threads. Since restart logs are kept in conventional flat files, reading the data in a binary format at high rates is not a problem. Likewise, since the cache is kept in memory, updating the cache at more than a million updates per second is likewise not a major problem.

The only remaining issue is to arrange for only one TSD to write each row to the database. This can be done by having each TSD pick a random time to wait before writing an idle dirty row back to the database. When the TSD starts the write, it will write a start transaction to the log, and when it completes the write, it will write a finish transaction to the log. When other TSDs read the finish transaction from the first TSD's restart log, they will silently discard the dirty row if their last update time matches the update time that was written to the database. Any TSD that reads a start transaction will delay its own write time for that row by a few seconds to allow the finish operation to arrive. By setting the range of the random times large with respect to the time required to propagate the start transaction, the probability that two TSDs will start a write on the same row can be made very, very small. Even if two TSDs do decide to write the same row to the database, row updates are atomic, so the two processes will write the same data (since the row is idle at this point). The net effect is that each row will almost always be written to the database only once, on average.

With an understanding of basic concepts related to building a large scale, NoSQL time series database provided by Chapter 3 and the exploration of open source tools to implement those ideas, as described here in Chapter 4, you should now be well prepared to tackle your own project with time series data. But before you do, consider how one of the options described here can fix a problem you might not yet know exists. Chapter 5 shows you how.

Solving a Problem You Didn't Know You Had

Whenever you build a system, it's good practice to do testing before you begin using it, especially before it goes into production. If your system is designed to store huge amounts of time series data—such as two years' worth of sensor data—for critical operations or analysis, it's particularly important to test it. The failure of a monitoring system for drilling or pump equipment on an oil rig, for manufacturing equipment, medical equipment, or an airplane, can have dire consequences in terms financial loss and physical damage, so it is essential that your time series data storage engine is not only high performance, but also robust. Sometimes people do advance testing on a small data sample, but tests at this small scale are not necessarily reliable predictors of how your system will function at scale. For serious work, you want a serious test, using full-scale data. But how can you do that?

The Need for Rapid Loading of Test Data

Perhaps you have preexisting data for a long time range that could be used for testing, and at least you can fairly easily build a program to generate synthetic data to simulate your two years of information. Either way, now you're faced with a problem you may not have realized you have: if your system design was already pushing the limits on data ingestion to handle the high-velocity data expected in production, how will you deal with loading two years' worth of such data in a reasonable time? If you don't want to have to wait two years to perform the test, you must either give up having a full-scale test by downsampling or you must find a clever way to speed up test data ingestion rates enormously compared with normal production rates. For this example, to ingest two years of data in a day or two, you will need to ingest test data 100–1,000 times faster than your production rate. Even if your production data ingestion rate is only moderately high, your test data ingestion rate is liable to need to be outrageous. We choose the option to speed up the ingestion rate for test data. That's where the open source code extensions developed by MapR (described in Chapter 4) come to the rescue.

Using Blob Loader for Direct Insertion into the Storage Tier

The separate blob loader described in Chapter 4 (see Figure 4-3) is ideal for ingesting data to set up a test at scale. The blob loader design has been shown to provide more than 1,000-fold acceleration of data loading over the rate achieved by unmodified Open TSDB's hybrid wide table/blob design as shown in Figure 4-1. The advantages of this direct-insertion approach are especially apparent when you imagine plotting the load times for the different approaches, as shown in Figure 5-1.

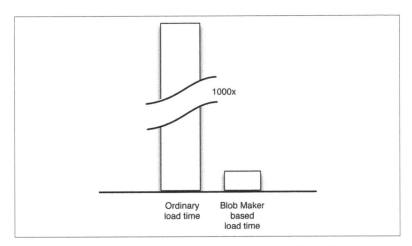

1000x

Ordinary
load time

Blob Maker
based
load time

Figure 5-1. Load times for large-scale test data can be prohibitive with the hybrid-style format (point-by-point + blob) produced by ordinary Open TSDB (left), but this problem is solved with rapid ingestion rates obtained by using the open source code extensions to do direct blob insertion (right).

There are other situations in which direct blob insertion can be beneficial as well, but even by just making it practical to do realistic testing at scale of a critical time series database, this approach can have wide impact.

CHAPTER 6

Time Series Data in Practical Machine Learning

With the increasing availability of large-scale data, machine learning is becoming a common tool that businesses use to unlock the potential value in their data. There are several factors at work to make machine learning more accessible, including the development of new technologies and practical approaches.

Many machine-learning approaches are available for application to time series data. We've already alluded to some in this book and in *Practical Machine Learning: A New Look at Anomaly Detection* (*http://bit.ly/anomaly_detection*), an earlier short book published by O'Reilly. In that book, we talked about how to address basic questions in anomaly detection, especially how determine what normal looks like, and how to detect deviations from normal.

Keep in mind that with anomaly detection, the machine-learning model is trained offline to learn what normal is and to set an adaptive threshold for anomaly alerts. Then new data, such as sensor data, can be assessed to determine how similar the new data is to what the model expects. The degree of mismatch to the model expectations can be used to trigger an alert that signals apparent faults or discrepancies as they occur. Sensor data is a natural fit to be collected and stored as a time series database. Sensors on equipment or system logs for servers can generate an enormous amount of time-based data, and with new technologies such as the Apache Hadoop–based NoSQL systems described in this book, it is now feasible to save months or even years of such data in time series databases.

But is it worthwhile to do so?

Predictive Maintenance Scheduling

Let's consider a straightforward but very important example to answer this question. Suppose a particular piece of critically important equipment is about to fail. You would like to be able to replace the part *before* a costly disaster.

Failure Prediction at Work in the Movie "2001, A Space Odyssey"

Hal	Sorry to interrupt the festivities, Dave, but I think we've got a problem.
Bowman	What is it, Hal?
Hal	MY F.P.C. shows an impending failure of the antenna orientation unit.
Hal	The A.O. unit should be replaced within the next 72 hours.

It would be good if you could see signs leading up to the failure so that you could do preventive maintenance. If the piece is something such as a wind turbine, a pump in a drilling rig, or a component of a jet engine such as the one shown in Figure 6-1, the consequences of the failure can be dire. Part of the problem is that you may not know what to watch for. That's where a retrospective study can help.

Figure 6-1. Predictive maintenance scheduling—replacing parts be-
fore a serious problem occurs—is a huge benefit in systems with ex
pensive and highly critical equipment such as this turbine inside a jet
engine.

If you keep good, detailed long-term histories of maintenance on essential components of equipment down to the level of the part number,
location, dates it went into use, notes on wear, and the dates of any
failures, you may be able to reconstruct the events or conditions that
led up to failures and thus build a model for how products wear out,
or you may find predictive signs or even the cause of impending trouble. This type of precise, long-term maintenance history is not a time
series, but coupled with a time series database of sensor data that records operating conditions, you have a powerful combination to unlock the insights you need. You can correlate the observations your
sensors have made for a variety of parameters during the days, weeks,
or months leading up to the part failure or up to an observed level of
wear that is disturbing. This pattern of retrospective machine learning
analysis on the combination of a detailed maintenance history and a
long-term time series database has widespread applicability in transportation, manufacturing, health care, and more.

Why do you need to go to the trouble of saving the huge amount of time series sensor data for long time ranges, such as years, rather than perhaps just a month? It depends of course on your particular situation and what the opportunity cost of not being able to do this style of predictive maintenance may be. But part of the question to ask yourself is: what happens if you only save a month of sensor data at a time, but the critical events leading up to a catastrophic part failure happened six weeks or more before the event? Maybe temperatures exceeded a safe range or an outside situation caused an unusual level of vibration in the component for a short time two months earlier. When you try to reconstruct events before the failure or accident, you may not have the relevant data available any more. This situation is especially true if you need to look back over years of performance records to understand what happened in similar situations in the past.

The better alternative is to make use of the tools described in this report so that it is practical to keep much longer time spans for your sensor data along with careful maintenance histories. In the case of equipment used in jet aircraft, for instance, it is not only the airline that cares about a how equipment performs at different points in time and what the signs of wear or damage are. Some manufacturers of important equipment also monitor ongoing life histories of the parts they produce in order to improve their own design choices and to maintain quality.

Manufacturers are not only concerned with collecting sensor data to monitor how their equipment performs in factories during production; they also want to manufacture smart equipment that reports on its own condition as it is being used by the customer. The manufacturer can include a service to monitor and report on the status of a component in order to help the customer optimize function through tuning. This might involve better fuel consumption, for example. These "smart parts" are of more value than mute equipment, so they may give the manufacturer a competitive edge in the marketplace, not to mention the benefits they provide the customer who purchases them.

The benefits of this powerful combination of detailed maintenance histories plus long-term time series databases of sensor data for machine learning models can, in certain, industries, be enormous.

CHAPTER 7

Advanced Topics for Time Series Databases

So far, we have considered how time series can be stored in databases where each time series is easily identified: possibly by name, possibly by a combination of tagged values. The applications of such time series databases are broad and cover many needs.

There are situations, however, where the time series databases that we have described so far fall short. One such situation is where we need to have a sense of location in addition to time. An ordinary time series database makes the assumption that essentially all queries will have results filtered primarily based on time. Put another way, time series databases require to you specify *which* metric and *when* the data was recorded. Sometimes, however, we need to include the concept of *where*. We may want to specify only *where* and *when* without specifying *which*. When we make this change to the queries that we want to use, we move from having a time series database to having a geo-temporal database.

Note that it isn't the inclusion of locational data into a time series database per se that makes it into a geo-temporal database. Any or all of latitude, longitude, *x*, *y*, or *z* could be included in an ordinary time series database without any problem. As long as we know which time series we want and what time range we want, this locational data is just like any other used to identify the time series. It is the requirement that location data be a *primary part of querying the database* that makes all the difference.

Suppose, for instance, that we have a large number of data-collecting robots wandering the ocean recording surface temperature (and a few other parameters) at various locations as they move around. A natural query for this data is to retrieve all temperature measurements that have been made within a specified distance of a particular point in the ocean. With an ordinary time series database, however, we are only able to scan by a particular robot for a particular time range, yet we cannot know which time to search for to find the measurements for a robot at a particular location—we don't have any way to build an efficient query to get the data we need, and it's not practical to scan the entire database. Also, because the location of each robot changes over time, we cannot store the location in the tags for the entire time series. We can, however, solve this problem by creating a geo-temporal database, and here's how.

Somewhat surprisingly, it is possible to implement a geo-temporal database using an ordinary time series database together with just a little bit of additional machinery called a geo-index. That is, we can do this if the data we collect and the queries we need to do satisfy a few simple assumptions. This chapter describes these assumptions, gives examples of when these assumptions hold, and describes how to implement this kind of geo-temporal database.

Stationary Data

In the special case where each time series is gathered in a single location that does not change, we do not actually need a geo-temporal database. Since the location doesn't change, the location does not need to be recorded more than once and can instead be recorded as an attribute of the time series itself, just like any other attribute. This means that querying such a database with a region of interest and a time range involves nothing more than finding the time series that are in the region and then issuing a normal time-based query for those time series.

Wandering Sources

The case of time series whose data source location changes over time is much more interesting than the case where location doesn't change. The exciting news is that if the data source location changes relatively slowly, such as with the ocean robots, there are a variety of methods to make location searches as efficient as time scans. We describe only one method here.

To start with, we assume that all the locations are on a plane that is divided into squares. For an ocean robot, imagine its path mapped out as a curve, and we've covered the map with squares. The robot's path will pass through some of the squares. Where the path crosses a square is what we call an intersection.

We also assume that consecutive points in a time series are collected near one another geographically because the data sources move slowly with respect to how often they collect data. As data is ingested, we can examine the location data for each time series and mark down in a separate table (the geo-index) exactly when the time series path intersects each square and which squares it intersects. These intersections of time series and squares can be stored and indexed by the ID of the square so that we can search the geo-index using the square and get a list of all intersections with that square. That list of intersections tells us which robots have crossed the square and when they crossed it. We can then use that information to query the time series database portion of our geo-temporal database because we now know *which* and *when*.

Figure 7-1 shows how this might work with relatively coarse partitioning of spatial data. Two time series that wander around are shown. If we want to find which time series might intersect the shaded circle and when, we can retrieve intersection information for squares A, B, C, D, E, and F. To get the actual time series data that overlaps with the circle, we will have to scan each segment of the time series to find out if they actually do intersect with the circle, but we only have to scan the segments that overlapped with one of these six squares.

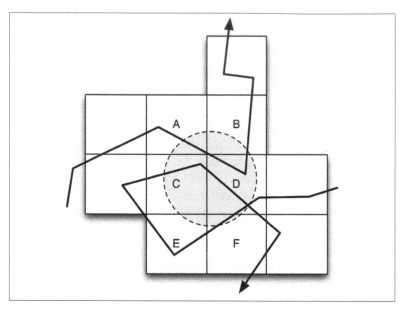

Figure 7-1. To find time windows of series that might intersect with the shaded circle, we only have to check segments that intersect with the six squares A–F. These squares involve considerably more area than we need to search, but in this case, only three segments having no intersection with the circle would have to be scanned because they intersect squares A–F. This means that we need only scan a small part of the total data in the time series database.

If we make the squares smaller like in Figure 7-2, we will have a more precise search that forces us to scan less data that doesn't actually overlap with the circle. This is good, but as the squares get smaller, the number of data points in the time series during the overlap with each square becomes smaller and smaller. This makes the spatial index bigger and ultimately decreases efficiency.

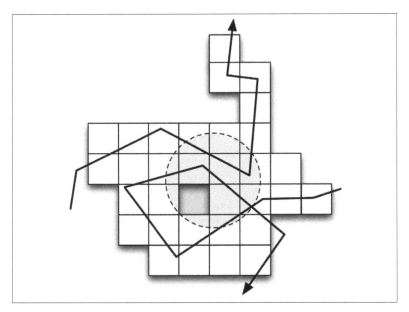

Figure 7-2. With smaller squares, we have more squares to check, but they have an area closer to that of the circle of interest. The circle now intersects 13 squares, but only 2 segments with no intersection will be scanned, and those segments are shorter than before because the squares are smaller.

It is sometimes not possible to find a universal size of square that works well for all of the time series in the database. To avoid that problem, you can create an adaptive spatial index in which intersections are recorded at the smallest scale square possible that still gives enough samples in the time series segment to be efficient. If a time series involves slow motion, a very fine grid will be used. If the time series involves faster motion, a coarser grid will be used. A time series that moves quickly sometimes and more slowly at other times will have a mix of fine and coarse squares. In a database using a blobbed storage format, a good rule of thumb is to record intersections at whichever size square roughly corresponds a single blob of data.

Space-Filling Curves

As a small optimization, you can label the squares in the spatial index according to a pattern known as a Hilbert curve, as shown in Figure 7-3. This labeling is recursively defined so that finer squares share the prefix of their label with overlapping coarser squares. Another nice property of Hilbert labeling is that roughly round or square regions will overlap squares with large runs of sequential labels. This can mean that a database such as Apache HBase that orders items according to their key may need to do fewer disk seeks when finding the content associated with these squares.

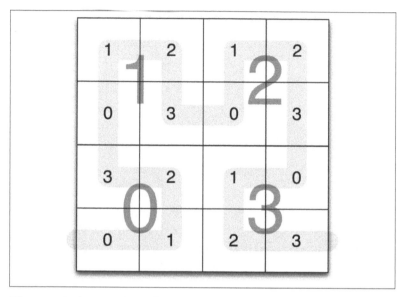

Figure 7-3. A square can be recursively divided into quarters and labeled in such a way that the roughly round regions will overlap squares that are nearly contiguous. This ordering can make retrieving the contents associated with each square fast in a database like HBase or MapR-DB because it results in more streaming I/O. This labeling is recursively defined and is closely related to the Hilbert curve.

Whether or not this is an important optimization will depend on how large your geo-index of squares is. Note that Hilbert labeling of squares does not change how the time series themselves are stored, only how the index of squares that is used to find intersections is stored. In many modern systems, the square index will be small enough to fit in memory. If so, Hilbert labeling of the squares will be an unnecessary inconvenience.

CHAPTER 8

What's Next?

The shape of the data landscape has changed, and it's about to undergo an even bigger upheaval. New technologies have made it reasonable and cost effective to collect and analyze *much* larger amounts of data, including time series data. That change, in turn, has enticed people to greatly expand where, how, and how much data they want to collect. It isn't just about having data at a much larger scale to do the things we used to do at higher frequency, such as tracking stock trades in fractions of seconds or measuring residential energy usage every few minutes instead of once a month. The combination of greatly increasing scale plus emerging technologies to collect and analyze data for valuable insights is creating the desire and ability to do *new* things.

This ability to try something new raises the question: what's next? Before we take a look forward, let's review the key ideas we have covered so far.

A New Frontier: TSDBs, Internet of Things, and More

The way we watch the world is new. Machine sensors "talk to" servers and machines talk to each other. Analysts collect data from social media for sentiment analysis to find trends and see if they correlate to the behavior of stock trading. Robots wander across the surface of the oceans, taking repeated measurements of a variety of parameters as they go. Manufacturers not only monitor manufacturing processes for fine-tuning of quality control, they also produce "smart parts" as components of high-tech equipment to report back on their function from the field. The already widespread use of sensor data is about to vastly expand as creative companies find new ways to deploy sensors, such as embedding them into fabric to make "smart clothes" to monitor parameters including heart function. There are also many wearable devices for reporting on a person's health and activity. One of the most widespread sources of machine data already in action is from system logs in data center monitoring. As techniques such as those described in this report become widely known, more and more people are choosing to collect data as time series. Going forward, where will you find time series data? The answer is: essentially everywhere.

These types of sensors take an enormous number of measurements, which raises the issue of how to make use of the enormous influx of data they produce. New methods are needed to deal with the entire time series pipeline from sensor to insight. Sensor data must be collected at the site of measurement and communicated. Transport technologies are needed to carry this information to the platform used for central storage and analysis. That's where the methods for scalable time series databases come in. These new TSDB technologies lie at the heart of the IoT and more.

This evolution is natural—doing new things calls for new tools, and time series databases for very large-scale datasets are important tools. Services are emerging to provide technology that is custom designed to handle large-scale time series data typical of sensor data. In this book, however, we have focused on how to build your own time series database, one that is cost effective and provides excellent performance at high data rates and very large volume.

We recommend using Apache Hadoop–based NoSQL platforms— such as Apache HBase or MapR-DB—for building large-scale, nonrelational time series databases because of their scalability and the efficiency of data retrieval they provide for time series data. When is that the right solution? In simple terms, a time series database is the right choice when you have a very large amount of data that requires a scalable technology and when the queries you want to make are mainly based on a time span.

New Options for Very High-Performance TSDBs

We've described some open source tools and new approaches to build large-scale time series databases. These include open source tools such as Open TSDB, code extensions to modify Open TSDB that were developed by MapR, and a convenient user interface called Grafana that works with Open TSDB.

The design of the data workflow, data format, and table organization all affect performance of a time series database. Data can be loaded into wide tables in a point-by-point manner in a NoSQL-style, non-relational storage tier for better performance and scalability as compared to a traditional relational database schema with one row per data point. For even faster retrieval, a hybrid table design can be achieved with a data flow that retrieves data from wide table for compression into blobs and reloads the table with row compaction. Unmodified Open TSDB produces this hybrid-style storage tier. To greatly improve the rate of ingestion, you can make use of the new open source extensions developed by MapR to enable direct blob insertion. This style also solves the problem of how to quickly ingest sufficient data to carry out a test of a very large volume database. This novel design has achieved rates as high as 100 million data points a second, a stunning advancement.

We've also described some of the ways in which time series data is useful in practical machine learning. For example, models based on the combination of a time series database for sensor measurements and long-term, detailed maintenance histories make it possible to do predictive maintenance scheduling. This book also looked at the advanced topic of building a geo-temporal database.

Looking to the Future

What's next? The sky's the limit…and so is the ocean, the farm, your cell phone, the stock market, medical nano-sensors implanted in your body, and possibly the clothes you are wearing. We started our discussion with some pioneering examples of extremely valuable insights discovered through patterns and trends in time series data. From the Winds and Current Charts of Maury and the long-term environmental monitoring started by Keeling with his CO_2 measurements to the modern exploration of our planet by remote sensors, time series data has been shown to be a rich resource. And now, as we move into uncharted waters of new invention, who knows where the journey will take us?

The exciting thing is that by building the fundamental tools and approaches described here, the foundation is in place to support innovations with time series data. The rest is up to your imagination.

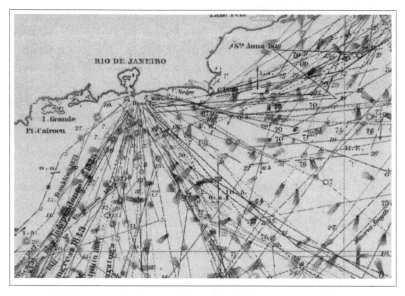

Figure 8-1. An excerpt from Maury's Wind and Current Charts that were based on time series data. These charts were used by ship captains to optimize their routes.

Resources

Tools for Working with NoSQL Time Series Databases

1. OpenTSDB (*http://opentsdb.net/*)
2. Open source MapR extensions (*https://github.com/mapr-demos/opentsdb*)
3. Grafana (*http://grafana.org/*)
4. Apache HBase (*http://hbasc.apache.org/*)
5. MapR DB (*https://www.mapr.com/products/m7*)
6. Blog on very high-performance test with Open TSDB and MapR extensions (*http://bit.ly/1s3wkmp*)

More Information About Use Cases Mentioned in This Book

1. Maury's Wind and Current Charts (*http://icoads.noaa.gov/maury.pdf*)
2. Old Weather project (*http://www.oldweather.org/*)
3. Keeling CO_2 Curve (*http://bit.ly/1qNY3oZ*)
4. Liquid Robotics (*http://liquidr.com/*)
5. Planet OS (*https://planetos.com/*)

Additional O'Reilly Publications by Dunning and Friedman

1. Practical Machine Learning: Innovations in Recommendation (*http://oreil.ly/1qt7riC*) (February 2014)
2. Practical Machine Learning: A New Look at Anomaly Detection (*http://oreil.ly/1qNqKm2*) (June 2014)

About the Authors

Ted Dunning is Chief Applications Architect at MapR Technologies and active in the open source community, being a committer and PMC member of the Apache Mahout, Apache ZooKeeper, and Apache Drill projects, and serving as a mentor for these Apache projects: Storm, Flink, Optiq, Datafu, and Drill. He has contributed to Mahout clustering, classification, matrix decomposition algorithms, and the new Mahout Math library, and recently designed the t-digest algorithm used in several open source projects. He also architected the modifications for Open TSDB described in this book.

Ted was the chief architect behind the MusicMatch (now Yahoo Music) and Veoh recommendation systems, built fraud-detection systems for ID Analytics (LifeLock), and has issued 24 patents to date. Ted has a PhD in computing science from University of Sheffield. When he's not doing data science, he plays guitar and mandolin. Ted is on Twitter at *@ted_dunning*.

Ellen Friedman is a solutions consultant and well-known speaker and author, currently writing mainly about big data topics. She is a committer for the Apache Mahout project and a contributor to the Apache Drill project. With a PhD in Biochemistry, she has years of experience as a research scientist and has written about a variety of technical topics including molecular biology, nontraditional inheritance, and oceanography. Ellen is also co-author of a book of magic-themed cartoons, *A Rabbit Under the Hat*. Ellen is on Twitter at *@Ellen_Friedman*.

Colophon

The text font is Adobe Minion Pro; the heading font is Adobe Myriad Condensed; and the code font is Dalton Maag's Ubuntu Mono.